Our Ecosystems

Using Nonfiction to Promote Literacy Across the Curriculum

by Doris Roettger

Fearon Teacher Aids

A Paramount Communications Company

Teacher Consultants

Virginia Slachman
Cincinnati, Ohio

Joceyln Riley
Pinetop, Arizona

Editorial Director: Virginia L. Murphy

Editor: Virginia Massey Bell

Copyeditor: Kristin Eclov

Illustration: Anita Nelson

Design: Terry McGrath

Cover Design: Lucyna Green

Production: Rebecca Speakes

ISBN 0-86653-936-0

Printed in the United States of America
1. 9 8 7 6 5 4 3 2

A Note from the Author

$\mathcal{S}$tudents have a natural curiosity about the world in which they live. They are intensely interested in learning about real things, real places, and real people. They also enjoy and learn from hands-on experiences. Nonfiction books and magazines provide opportunities for students to explore their interests and extend their base of knowledge.

Reading nonfiction materials is different from reading fiction. To be effective readers, students need to learn how to locate the information they want to answer their questions. They also need to learn to think about and evaluate the accuracy of the information presented. Finally, they need opportunities to learn the relationship between what they read and the activities in which they apply their new knowledge.

You, as the teacher, can provide opportunities for students to learn from their observations, their reading, and their writing in an integrated language-arts approach across the curriculum.

Modeling thinking strategies and then providing practice across the curriculum will help students become observers and explorers of their world, plus effective users of literacy skills. Encouraging students to extend and demonstrate their understanding through a variety of communication areas—speaking, reading, drama, writing, listening, and art—is also very valuable.

The suggestions in this guide are action-oriented and designed to involve students in the thinking process. The activities do not relate to any one single book. Instead, the strategies and activities are designed to be used with any of the books suggested in the bibliography or with books found in your own media center. The suggested interdisciplinary activities can also be used across grade levels.

Each lesson begins by reading a nonfiction book, book chapter, or magazine article to the class that relates to the follow-up activities you select. During the activity phase and at other class times, students are encouraged to return to the nonfiction selections available in the classroom to find answers to their questions, compare and verify their observations, and add new information to their current knowledge base.

The individual theme units are designed to be used for any length of time from a few days to a month or more, depending on the needs and interests of your students.

Suggested goals for this unit are provided near the beginning of this guide on page 18. The webs on pages 7–9 give you an overview of the areas in which activities are provided.

On each page of this guide, there is space for you to write reflective notes as well as ideas that you want to remember for future teaching. This guide is designed to be a rich resource from which you make the decisions and then select the learning experiences that will be the most appropriate for your students.

Doris Roettger

Contents

Literacy Skills

*T*he following literacy skills are addressed in
Our Ecosystems theme guide.

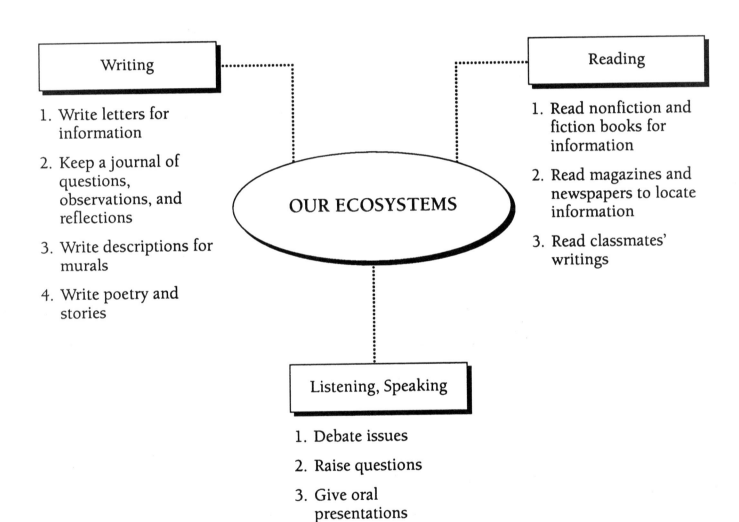

Writing

1. Write letters for information

2. Keep a journal of questions, observations, and reflections

3. Write descriptions for murals

4. Write poetry and stories

OUR ECOSYSTEMS

Reading

1. Read nonfiction and fiction books for information

2. Read magazines and newspapers to locate information

3. Read classmates' writings

Listening, Speaking

1. Debate issues

2. Raise questions

3. Give oral presentations

Integrated Curriculum

$\mathcal{T}$he following interdisciplinary areas are addressed in *Our Ecosystems* theme guide.

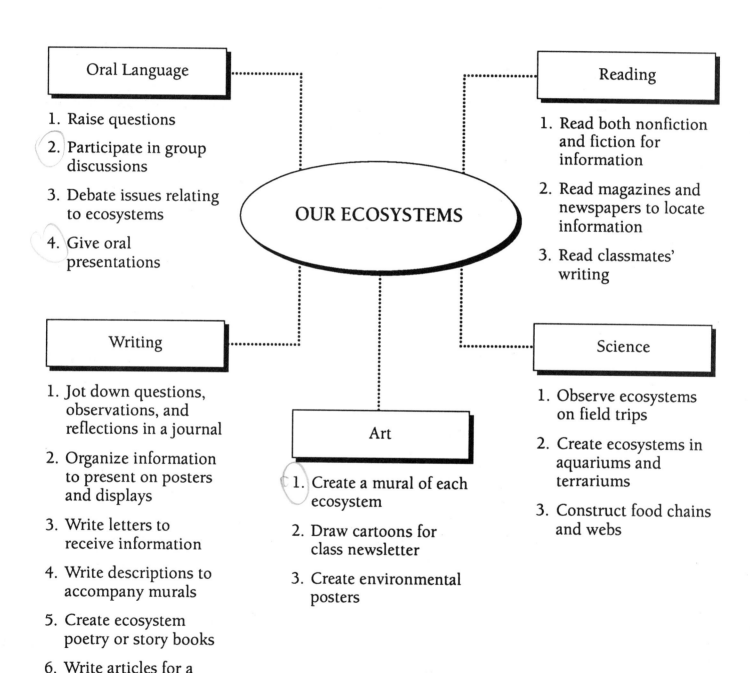

Oral Language

1. Raise questions
2. Participate in group discussions
3. Debate issues relating to ecosystems
4. Give oral presentations

Reading

1. Read both nonfiction and fiction for information
2. Read magazines and newspapers to locate information
3. Read classmates' writing

OUR ECOSYSTEMS

Writing

1. Jot down questions, observations, and reflections in a journal
2. Organize information to present on posters and displays
3. Write letters to receive information
4. Write descriptions to accompany murals
5. Create ecosystem poetry or story books
6. Write articles for a class newsletter

Art

1. Create a mural of each ecosystem
2. Draw cartoons for class newsletter
3. Create environmental posters

Science

1. Observe ecosystems on field trips
2. Create ecosystems in aquariums and terrariums
3. Construct food chains and webs

Learning and Working Strategies

*T*he following learning and working strategies are addressed in *Our Ecosystems* theme guide.

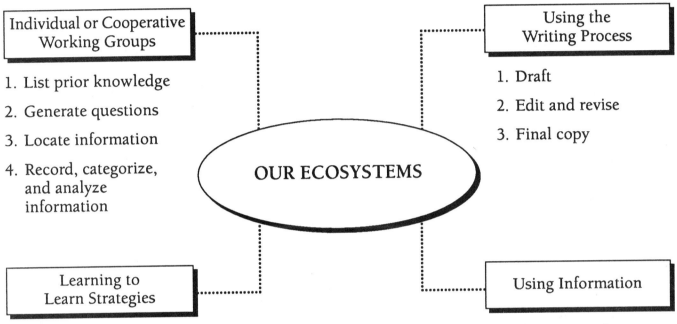

Individual or Cooperative Working Groups

1. List prior knowledge
2. Generate questions
3. Locate information
4. Record, categorize, and analyze information

Using the Writing Process

1. Draft
2. Edit and revise
3. Final copy

OUR ECOSYSTEMS

Learning to Learn Strategies

1. Replicate ecosystems
2. Observe interdependence of plants, bugs, insects, and animals in a variety of ecosystems
3. Read nonfiction books, magazines, and newspapers to locate answers to questions
4. Use vocabulary related to ecosystems
5. Organize information
6. Reflect on observations using the senses
7. Compare ecosystems
8. Summarize information and draw conclusions on the basis of analysis

Using Information

1. Create murals
2. Create cartoons
3. Write a newsletter
4. Write poetry and story books
5. Give oral presentations

About Ecosystems

The Earth supports a variety of ecosystems, including desert, forest, tundra, ocean, grasslands, and wetlands. An ecosystem refers to a group of plants and animals that live in a certain area and that depend on one another for survival. Each ecosystem has its own set of unique characteristics, such as climate, plant and animal species, terrain, and environmental problems. Habitat, on the other hand, specifically refers to where a particular plant or animal lives within a specific ecosystem. The relationship between plants, animals, and their environment is so closely connected that one change can affect an entire ecosystem. The following ecosystems are studied in this guide:

Deserts

About one-seventh of the Earth's land surface is currently considered desert. Due to environmental changes, the world's deserts are continually expanding. Many deserts receive less than 10 inches of moisture a year. They can be located in very cold or very warm climates. Even though the desert is a very harsh environment, many plants and animals adapt to the climate and even thrive there.

Forests

About 30% of the Earth's land is covered with natural forests. Forests are natural resources and are vital to all living things. Trees absorb carbon dioxide, produce oxygen, prevent erosion, help build soil, provide homes and food for birds and animals, and provide ingredients for medicines. There are four major types of forests—tropical rainforests, temperate rainforests, coniferous forests, and deciduous forests. It may take hundreds of years for trees to grow to maturity and become part of old growth in a forest. Tropical rainforests are self-sustaining ecosystems producing their own nutrients and climate. About one-quarter of all prescription drugs come from rainforest plants, as well as many popular fruits. Forests of all kinds are being threatened by the activities of people. Most of the deforestation has taken place during the 20th century. When forests are lost, all living things are affected. Each of us has a responsibility to see that forests are protected.

Oceans

The four oceans of the world—Atlantic, Pacific, Indian, and Arctic—cover about 70% of the Earth's surface. This is approximately forty times the size of the United States. The average ocean is approximately two and a half miles deep. The ocean ecosystem also includes smaller bodies of water, including seas, bays, and gulfs. Oceans are composed of salt water, even though most of the water that flows into them is from the world's fresh water rivers. Some of the richest marine ecosystems are in estuaries or wetlands, where ocean and land meet. Oceans are never still—they are constantly moving due to waves, winds, tides, earthquakes, and currents. There are a number of ecosystems in the oceans. Approximately 90% of all marine life can be found in the shallow water above the continental shelf. Most of the animals that live in the oceans are invertebrates, not fish. A variety of plants and animals live at different ocean depths. Plants are critical to all marine life. The most important sea plant is called *phytoplankton*. About 70% of all photosynthesis that takes place on Earth is produced by phytoplankton. Overfishing and toxic wastes from industry, sewage, and agriculture are responsible for a recent decline in many marine species.

Prairies and Grasslands

Grasslands, also known as prairies or savanas, are located throughout North America, South America, Asia, Africa, and Australia. Grasslands are often viewed as large expanses of land covered with tall grasses. Prairies fall somewhere between forests and deserts because they do not receive enough precipitation to support large trees and too much precipitation for desert vegetation. The grasslands have many diverse ecosystems. Almost all of the native grasslands in the United States have been plowed under and developed for agricultural purposes.

Tundra

The treeless plains of the Arctic Circle are called *the tundra*. The temperature range in the tundra is less than 0° C most of the year and never rises above 10° C. A thin layer of soil covers the permafrost—ground that stays frozen all year long. Plants that thrive on the tundra in spring and summer must have shallow, but large, root systems in order to take advantage of the nutrients and water within the thin soil layer.

Wetlands

Wetlands are regions that contain permanent moisture, such as swamps, marshes, estuaries, bogs, ponds, and lakes. Some wetlands are swamps or marshes located near the ocean and contain only salt water. Other marshes or bogs located near forests contain fresh water. Wetlands that contain both fresh water and salt water are called *estuaries* and are located along coastal regions where the ocean meets a river or stream. Wetlands have many important functions. They help clean our water by filtering sediments. Wetlands also support a variety of species of vegetation, which helps in slowing seasonal flooding. The wetlands protect the land against excessive erosion because wetland vegetation helps keep soil stable and in place. Wetlands provide homes for birds, fish, animals, and insects. Shellfish, fish, and lumber are harvested from some wetlands. Lakes and rivers can also be grouped under the wetlands ecosystems. So can ponds, which are warmer than rivers and lakes, because ponds are smaller and more shallow.

Suggested Reading Selections

A variety of nonfiction and fiction selections for the intermediate grades is suggested for use with this theme unit. You will probably want to assemble a collection of materials ahead of time. Or, you may wish to have the students help collect several titles from the library as a group activity. The number and type of selections you and the students read will depend on the length of time you devote to this unit, as well as the availability of the titles.

Nonfiction Books

DESERTS

Deserts by Oliver Twist. New York, NY: Dillon Press, 1991. Describes many plants, insects, reptiles, mammals, and birds found in deserts around the world. Includes a brief description of the lifestyle of the desert people in Australia and southern Africa and their attempts to raise crops in the desert. Includes beautiful color photographs, maps, and diagrams.

A Desert Year by Carol Lerner. New York, NY: Morrow Junior Books, 1991. Organized by seasons of the year. Each page is devoted to a description of three or four plants or animals in the deserts of the southwestern United States. For each of the four seasons, the same categories are given, but different animals and plants are described. Beautiful water-color pictures show animals and plants in their separate ecosystems.

A Night and a Day in the Desert by Jennifer Owings Dewey. Boston, MA: Little, Brown & Company, 1991. Describes how each of the plants and animals survive the harsh environment of extreme heat and very little water over a 24-hour period of time. Reads like a story. Colorful illustrations on each page.

24 Hours in a Desert by Barrie Watts. New York, NY: Franklin Watts, 1991. Describes ways animals and plants use the environment to survive in the Sonora Desert in Arizona, California, and Mexico over a 24-hour period of time. Uses close-up color photography to show the flowers, cacti, birds, and animals. Has a caption for each photograph.

FORESTS

Ancient Forests by Alexandra Siy. New York, NY: Dillon Press, 1991. Describes the conifers of the old growth forests in the Pacific

Northwest. Shows the interdependence of plants, animals, and humans. Explores the value of the forests in our lives and ways that we can conserve the forests.

The Brazilian Rain Forest by Alexander Siy. New York, NY: Dillon Press, 1992. Each chapter is divided into short sections that are easy to read and understand. Explains the interdependence between some of the plants and insects and other animals.

Chico Mendes by Susan DeStefano. New York, NY: Twenty-First Century Books, 1992. Biography of Chico Mendes as a boy, as a rubber tapper, as a union leader, and as an environmentalist. Mendes made his living from the forest without harming the environment.

Earth's Vanishing Forests by Roy A. Gallant. New York, NY: Macmillan Publishing Company, 1991. Explores the reasons why people around the world are concerned about the loss of forests, particularly the rainforests. Gives a glimpse of how the destruction of the rainforests affects the lives of people who make the rainforest their home.

In the Forest by Jim Arnosky. New York, NY: Lothrop, Lee and Shepard Books, 1989. Book of eleven beautiful oil paintings of the forest with a brief, easy-to-read description of the animals, trees, and other plants opposite each painting.

Life in the Rainforests by Lucy Baker. New York, NY: Franklin Watts, 1990. Describes in short paragraphs the importance of rainforests and the types of plants and the animals that live there. Detailed captions accompany the photographs.

The Rainforest by Billy Goodman. New York, NY: Tern Enterprise, Inc., 1991. Describes the plants and animals found in the tropical rainforests. Explains how human activities can harm the fragile ecosystems.

Rain Forest by Barbara Taylor. New York, NY: Dorling Kindersley, 1992. Feature the animals or plants found in the rainforests. Much of the information is provided in detailed captions focusing on various parts of the plants and animals.

Tropical Rainforest by Michael Bright. New York, NY: Aladdin Books, 1991. Each section or chapter is one paragraph with captioned illustrations. Easy to read.

Tropical Rainforests by Jean Hamilton. San Luis Obispo, CA: Blake Publishing, 1990. Describes the plants and animals that can be found at each level of the rainforest. Includes interesting bits of information about some of the animals as well. Beautiful photographs on each page.

Tropical Rainforests Around the World by Elaine Landau. New York, NY: Franklin Watts, 1990. Short chapters on conditions needed by rainforests to support a variety of trees, plants, animals and birds, and insects. Explains why the rainforests are important. Photographs on most pages.

Vanishing Forests by Helen J. Challand. Chicago, IL: Childrens Press, 1991. Describes the animal and plant life that can be found in the ground area, the shrubs, the understory, and the canopy of both the rainforests and the temperate forests. Presents the value of forests and why they are being destroyed. Gives ways that everyone can take action for reforestation.

WETLANDS

Pond and River by Steve Parker. New York, NY: Alfred A. Knopf, 1988. A book of photographs with detailed captions of plants and animals found in ponds and rivers during the four seasons. Excellent resource for identifying plants and animal life.

Pond Life by Colin Milkins. New York, NY: The Bookwright Press, 1990. Describes the physical characteristics of water plants. Categorizes the animal life of a pond into herbivores and carnivores.

The Hidden Life of the Pond by David M. Schwartz. New York, NY: Crown Publishers, Inc., 1988. Describes the plants, insects, and animals found in a pond during each season. Large beautiful color photographs included.

Saving Our Wetlands and Their Wildlife by Karen Liptak. New York, NY: Franklin Watts, 1991. Describes different types of endangered plants and animals. Explains many of the environmental threats to the wetlands. Easy to read.

Wading into Wetlands by Judy Braus. Washington, DC: National Wildlife Federation, 1989. Activities and crafts related to the study of the wetlands. Elementary and Junior High level material.

OCEANS

Life on a Coral Reef by Lionel Bender. New York, NY: Glouster Press, 1989. Describes coral reefs and the different animals and plants that live on them. Tells how coral reefs form, what they look like, and what sorts of ecosystems develop around them.

The Living Ocean by Robert Mattson. Hillside, NJ: Enslow Publishers, Inc., 1991. Explores the ocean environment and the plants, fish, and mammals found there. Names the plants and animals that live in the ecosystems in the coastal area, offshore areas, and the polar, tropical, and deep ocean areas. Describes the value of each of these communities.

The Ocean by Anne Phillips. New York, NY: Crestwood House, 1990. Examines the ways the ocean is polluted. Presents scientific information in easy-to-understand language. Discusses the importance of the oceans and seashores to life on earth, the serious problems caused by pollution, and what can be done to prevent further damage.

Protecting the Oceans by John Baines. Austin, TX: Steck-Vaughn, 1991. Gives an overview of the importance of oceans. Describes mining, hunting, and fishing in the oceans. Short descriptions of various types of pollution and ways we can protect the oceans are also included. Numerous color photographs with captions. Easy to read.

Seas and Oceans by Clint Twist. New York, NY: Dillon Press, 1991. Takes a close look at some of the plants and animals found in the oceans of the world and the threats they face. Includes information on the Mediterranean Sea and the coral reefs in the tropical seas. Beautiful color photographs, maps, and diagrams are included.

GRASSLANDS AND TUNDRAS

Grasslands by David Lambert. Englewood Cliffs, NJ: Silver Burdett, 1988. Explores the different types of grasslands around the world. Also describes the differences in the development, climates, plant and animal life, as well as the exploitation and preservation of the various grasslands.

Grasslands and Tundra by Time-Life Books. Alexandria, VA: Time-Life Books, 1985. Describes grassland and tundra ecology.

Native Grasslands by Alexandra Siy. New York, NY: Dillon Press, 1991. Explores the animal and plant life in the prairie grasslands of North America and how they are related. Photographs are included.

Tundra, The Arctic Land by Bruce Hiscock. New York, NY: Atheneum, 1986. Describes the geography and the plants, animals, and people who have adapted to life on the Arctic tundra.

Fiction Books

Call of the Wild by Jack London. New York, NY: Grosset & Dunlap, 1931. A dog is forcibly taken to Alaska where he eventually becomes the leader of a wolf pack.

The Gift of the Sacred Dog by Paul Goble. Scarsdale, NY: Bradbury Press, 1980. A legend of how the horse came to the Plains Indians. Beautiful, bold illustrations.

The Goat in the Rug as told to Charles L. Blood and Martin A. Link by Geraldine. New York, NY: Macmillan Publishing, 1976. A goat named Geraldine explains how her Navajo friend, Glenmae, makes a rug from start to finish, using Geraldine's own wool. A delightful picturebook that gives some insight into how plants and animals are used in this part of the country.

The Island of the Blue Dolphins by Scott O'Dell. New York, NY: Dell, 1987. A courageous story of the survival of a young girl stranded alone on an island for eighteen years.

Julie of the Wolves by Jean Craighead George. New York, NY: HarperCollins, 1972. A young Eskimo girl is befriended by a pack of Arctic wolves as she travels on foot across the frozen North Slope of Alaska.

One Day in the Desert by Jean Craighead George. New York, NY: HarperCollins, 1983. Introduces the reader to the ecology of the desert by focusing on the interrelationships of the plants and animals in the desert during one July day. Uses a quasi-story structure.

One Day in the Prairie by Jean Craighead George. New York, NY: Thomas Y. Crowell, 1986. Describes the interdependence of the living community in the prairie—the complex food webs of birds and animals that eat grass and the animals that eat the grass eaters.

One Day in the Tropical Rain Forest by Jean Craighead George. New York, NY: Thomas Y. Crowell Junior Books, 1990. Tepui is determined to stop the bulldozers and trucks from destroying the rainforest, which is his home, and accepts the challenge of finding a nameless butterfly. Author takes reader on a journey through the lush rainforest.

One Day in the Woods by Jean Craighead George. New York, NY: Thomas Y. Crowell Junior Books, 1988. Rebecca climbs the highest tree in the Teatown Woods determined to find the ovenbird. Through the eyes of Rebecca, the author describes the relationships of the birds and animals in the northeastern deciduous forest.

Magazine Articles

"Lifelines in the Sand" from *Audubon*, 94: 34 - 35, July/August, 1992.

"The Big Thirst" from *Wildlife Conservation*, New York Zoological Society, July/August 1992.

" Our Disappearing Wetlands" from *National Geographic*, National Geographic Society, October 1992.

"Rebirth in the Prairie State (Restoration Projects in Illinois)" from *U. S. News & World Report*, May 18, 1992.

"A Restored Land" from *Sierra*, May/June, 1992.

"Wetlands, Water, Wildlife, Plants, and People" from *Science Scope*, National Science Teachers Association, September 1992.

National Geographic World, National Geographic Society, 17 & M Street NW, Washington, DC 20036. Published monthly for children ages 8-13. General information on a variety of topics concerning the natural world. Exceptional photography.

Instructional Goals

*I*nstructional goals for this theme unit are provided here. Space is also provided so that you may fill in your own individual goals where appropriate as well. By the end of this theme unit, students should be able to:

1. Define the word *ecosystem*.

2. Identify characteristics of deserts, forests, grasslands, oceans, ponds, tundra, and wetlands.

3. Create a pond ecosystem in an aquarium.

4. Create terrariums of various ecosystems.

5. Observe and identify microscopic pond animals.

6. Create a scale map of a forest ecosystem.

7. Identify various plants and animals within a given ecosystem.

8. Research and determine specific characteristics for survival in desert ecosystems.

9. Explain what a food chain is.

10. Explain what a food web is.

11. Write descriptions of rainforest plants and animals.

12. Create poetry and story books based on an ecosystem.

13. Write articles and draw cartoons for a classroom newsletter.

14. ....

15. ....

16. ....

17. ....

18. ....

19. ....

20. ....

Getting Started

Finding Out What Students Already Know and Raising Curiosity

The following activities are designed to help launch *Our Ecosystems* theme unit. You may want to use all of the activities or only one or two, depending on the needs of your students. At the beginning of each lesson, reading a nonfiction book or magazine selection to the class serves as a motivator and helps students become more familiar with and involved in using nonfiction selections. You'll also want to provide plenty of opportunities for students to return to nonfiction selections independently during the activity phases and at other times during class periods as well.

1. "Before, During, and After" Research Model

To help students better understand what they will research and learn from this unit, present a "Before, During, and After" research model to the class. Allow time for questions and answers about what students will be studying and learning. Encourage the students throughout the unit to brainstorm other ideas to add to each column of the model as well. Display the model in the classroom.

BEFORE	DURING	AFTER
Ecosystems Topic Introduced	*Search for Information*	*Using Information*
1. Observe ecosystems around school	1. Take field trips	1. Write newsletters
2. Transfer an ecosystem to the classroom	2. Observe interdependence in ecosystems	2. Create murals
3. List what is known	3. Read books, magazines, newspapers	3. Give oral presentations
4. Generate questions	4. View videos	
5. Identify resources for finding information	5. Listen to other students	
	6. Write for additional information	
	Construct Meaning	
	1. Take notes	
	2. Make graphic representations	
	3. Clarify points of confusion	
	4. Summarize	

2. Introducing Vocabulary

Introduce vocabulary as new words appear either in materials students are using or in classroom discussions. Encourage students to use the new words in their speaking and writing, when appropriate. Invite students to write new words on 3" x 5" index cards and post them around the room. A reproducible list of words and their definitions can be found on page 64.

a. Divide the class into small cooperative-working groups of four or five students. Help students in each group identify key words and concepts they think other students need to know as they study the Earth's ecosystems. Have students write each word on a 5" x 7" index card and draw or cut out a magazine picture that illustrates the meaning of each new word. Write a definition of each word on a second 5" x 7" index card. Post all the vocabulary words and definitions on a bulletin board in random order. Challenge students to match the words and definitions.

b. Provide time for groups of students to introduce one or two words a day to the class. Once words have been introduced, encourage students to use them in their speaking and writing throughout the day.

3. Investigating Ecosystems at School

a. You will need the following materials:

4 pegs or sticks per area to be observed

4 brightly colored flags or pieces of cloth per area

heavy string and scissors

magnifying glasses

journals and pencils

field reference books

large glass container to be used as a terrarium

sand and gravel to cover bottom of terrarium

small bits of charcoal

soil and grass or sand

piece of glass or screen to cover the top of the terrarium

containers for collecting live specimens

b. As a class, have students build a terrarium to match an outdoor environment of their choosing.

1. Cover the bottom of a large glass container with sand and gravel. Scatter small bits of charcoal on top of the sand and gravel. Cover with soil and grass or sand. If possible, make a terrarium for each type of environment the class investigates.

2. Divide the class into cooperative-working groups of four or five students. Have the groups of students measure five or more 2 ft. x 2 ft. outdoor areas. Some of the areas should be very close to trees, while others should be out in the open. For this activity, try to choose a time when the grass has not been mowed recently. Students should mark the corners of each area clearly with pegs or sticks and then tie heavy string around the pegged area. Tie brightly colored flags or pieces of cloth around each peg to mark the areas clearly.

3. Invite pairs of students within each group to observe the plants and insects they find in their assigned areas. Encourage the students to use magnifying glasses to get a closer look at the ecosystems. Have the students carefully collect one sample of each type of insect they see and put it into the terrarium. The insect should be released back into the environment after a short period of time.

4. Help students use reference books on plants and insects to identify the specimens that have been collected. Encourage the students to draw pictures of the insect specimens as well. Remind students to label their drawings. Then release the insects after they have been identified. Display the drawings around the terrariums.

5. About a week later, have another group of students observe the areas that have been staked out to see if they can find additional living creatures. Draw pictures and identify any new insect specimens. Display the new drawings in the classroom.

c. Hold a class meeting to identify all the plants and animals that can be found in the ecosystem area. Introduce the concept of ecosystems to the students by explaining that the groups of plants and animals that live in a certain area and depend on each other for survival are called *an ecosystem.*

d. Have students construct a large drawing of all the plants, birds, insects, and other animals that live in the ecosystem area identified.

4. At Home

Encourage students to mark an area in their yards or a nearby park and observe the plants and animals that live there. Remind students that they should obtain permission from the park or their parents before placing stakes in the ground. It is also important to tie brightly colored flags or pieces of cloth to each stake to prevent someone from walking or tripping into them. A magnifying glass is especially helpful for observing insects. Ask students to sketch what they see so they can share their observations with their classmates.

5. Sparking Interest

a. Encourage students to find out more information about the different ecosystems of the world. Spark interest in a variety of ecosystems by showing students the beautiful photographs in the many books listed in the suggested reading section as well as *National Geographic Magazines, World Magazines, Wildlife Conservation,* and other nature magazines. If possible, provide enough materials for each pair of students to have a book or magazine to look at. Encourage students to look for the variety of animals and plants in the different photographs. Record the students' responses on the chalkboard. Challenge students to identify the type of ecosystem the plants or animals might come from, such as forest, desert, grassland, and so on.

b. Encourage students to keep a journal throughout the ecosystems unit. Have students jot down in their journals what they know about the different ecosystems. As a class, create a web of what students already know. Categorize this information so that students begin to see how what they know fits together.

c. Encourage students to raise questions about different ecosystems. Write the questions on the chalkboard. As a class, try to categorize the questions according to the different ecosystems. Use the questions to create a web on a large sheet of butcher paper. Display the web where students can see the questions. As a whole group, identify sources of information where students can get their questions answered. Provide opportunities for students to do research to answer the questions.

6. Beginning the Research—Using the Table of Contents and Indexes to Locate Information

a. Divide the class into cooperative-working groups based on the ecosystems they are interested in.

b. Have each group locate several books pertaining to their area of study. Invite the students to look at the table of contents of the resource. As a class, discuss what information is available about each book from the table of contents. Encourage each group to record their information in their journals.

c. Ask each group to choose one question about their ecosystems and identify the key words in their questions. Have the students try to find information about the key words by looking the words up in an index in the back of one of the books. If students have difficulty identifying key words, hold a class meeting so either you or other groups of students can explain how to use the index for looking up information.

d. As students study the materials, encourage them to raise additional questions that can be added to the web discussed previously.

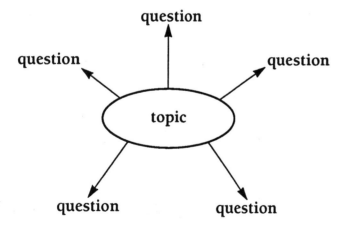

Real-Life Laboratory

Ponds, Wetlands, and Ocean Ecosystems

$\mathcal{T}$he activities in this section will heighten the students' awareness of ponds, wetlands, and ocean ecosystems. Select one or two books or articles on ponds, wetlands, or oceans to share with the class before students begin an activity.

1. Important and Interesting Information to Know

Write each of the following facts on cards and then post the cards around the room for students to read during free time. Encourage classroom discussion or debate about each or any of the statements.

Oceans

- Oceans receive most of their water from the world's rivers.

- The four oceans cover about 70% of the Earth. Oceans cover an area about forty times the size of the United States and average about two and a half miles in depth.

- Oceans are salt water, but the rivers that flow into them are fresh water.

- A variety of plants and animals live at different depths in the ocean.

- In the seas and oceans, plants are key to all other life forms. The most important sea plant is phytoplankton. About 70% of all photosynthesis that takes place on Earth is carried out by these marine plants.

- About 90% of marine life can be found in the shallow water above the continental shelf.

- Most of the animals that live in the sea are invertebrates, not fish.

- Overfishing and toxic wastes from industry, sewage, and agriculture are responsible for a decline in many species of marine life.

Wetlands and Ponds

- Wetlands can be made of salt water or fresh water.

- Some wetlands are swamps or marshes located near an ocean and contain only salt water, others are in forests and contain fresh water.

- Wetlands are pieces of land that contain permanent moisture. They include bogs, marshes, swamps, estuaries, lakes, ponds, and rivers.

- Wetlands help clean our water by filtering sediments.

- Because they support vegetation, wetlands also prevent flooding.

- Wetlands provide homes for birds, fish, animals, and insects.

- Shellfish, fish, and timber are harvested from some wetland areas.

- Ponds are warmer than rivers and lakes.

- Ponds are smaller and shallower than lakes.

2. Exploring the Ecosystem of a Pond

Take a field trip to a nearby pond to collect pond water, soil, plants, and animals to create a pond ecosystem at school. You will need the following materials:

> clean ice-cream cartons or plastic dishes with lids
>
> long-handled kitchen strainers and fine mesh nets or a pair of clean pantyhose attached to a coat hanger
>
> magnifying glasses and hand-held microscopes
>
> field guides
>
> journals and pencils
>
> boots
>
> camera (optional)

a. Ask students to sketch pictures of the pond and the area around it. Encourage students to show the trees, shrubs, plants, rocks, and any nearby buildings. This information can be used in subsequent writing and art activities.

b. Have students look for organisms under rocks or trees around the pond. Encourage students to use reference materials to help identify the animals and plants they see.

c. Have students look at the surface of the pond for floating plants or insects that live on the water's surface, such as water striders and boatmen.

d. To look at the microscopic animal life in the pond vegetation, take a fine net and gently push it through the vegetation in the pond, then jerk the handle slightly. This will knock the microscopic animal life into the net. Use a magnifying glass or hand-held microscope to look at the organisms in the net for a short time. If possible, have students draw pictures of the microscopic animals in their journals. Then gently place the net into the water and release the specimens back into the pond.

e. Collect pond water into a clean ice-cream carton or plastic dish with a lid. Ask students to watch carefully to see the tiny creatures.

f. If possible, use a long-handled kitchen strainer to scoop mud from the bottom of the pond. Have students use a magnifying glass to look for insect larvae.

g. Hold a class meeting to give students an opportunity to talk about what they observed and learned from their pond ecosystem.

3. Setting Up a Pond Water Aquarium

The items needed for this activity can be obtained on the field trip suggested in the above activity or volunteers can collect the samples over a weekend. You will need the following materials for setting up a pond water aquarium in the classroom:

> large glass container to be used for an aquarium
>
> pond water
>
> pond plants

pond insects

frog

magnifying glasses

microscopes and slides

Procedure:

a. Pour pond water into the aquarium. Add the pond plants to the aquarium so the tiny animals will have a food source. The plants will also produce oxygen in the water. You will probably have more success with a smaller number of organisms than a larger number. Do not add any tap water to the aquarium because the chlorine in the water may kill the specimens.

b. Have students use a hand-held microscope or magnifying glass to observe the movements of the tiny animals. Challenge students to observe what the animals eat, how they move, and watch for the different varieties of organisms in the water. The students will have to watch very closely to see what the microscopic animals eat.

c. To identify the organisms, have several students very carefully pour a spoonful of pond water on a glass slide. Use a microscope or a hand-held lens to identify the microscopic animals. Students should try to identify as many creatures as possible by comparing them with photographs in resource books.

4. Visiting a National Seashore or Estuary

a. If you live near the ocean, find out about the estuaries in your areas. An estuary occurs when ocean meets fresh water rivers or streams that flow into it. Estuaries are marshes with a mixture of salt water and fresh water. Contact the state office of Coastal Zone Management for estuary locations in your area. Find out what problems the estuaries have and what is being done to protect them.

b. Visit a national seashore to learn more about the plants and animals and their habitats along the coasts. Take along field glasses and reference books to help identify plants and animals in the area.

5. Wetland Inhabitants

Remind students that wetlands can be made of salt water or fresh water and can occur in many different locations. Some wetlands are swamps or marshes located near an ocean, while others are located in forests. Encourage students to research on their own where the following wetland animals live. Have students identify the type of wetlands where each bird or animal makes its home.

alligator	moose
dragonflies	raccoons
bullfrogs	muskrats
egret	fiddler crabs
blue heron	bears

6. Study of a Wetland

Hold a class discussion about the importance of the wetlands. Remind students that wetlands filter our water, help prevent erosion and flooding, and provide homes for a large variety of plants and animals. Explain that food and timber come from wetlands, too. If possible, invite students to visit a special wetland area. Encourage students to identify the type of wetland and the plants, animals, birds, and insects that live there. Challenge students to find out the environmental problems that affect the welfare of this particular wetland and what can be done to help protect it. Some choices might include the following:

mangrove swamp

southern forested wetlands

marshes throughout the U.S.

salt marshes on the U.S. coasts

shrub wetlands throughout the U.S.

river wetlands

inland marshes

northern forested wetlands

7. Making Salt Water and Setting Up a Salt Water Aquarium

a. To set up a salt water aquarium, you will need the following basic equipment:

glass tank

aquarium heater

undergravel filter

thermometer

marine gravel

synthetic sea salt (available at aquarium stores)

air pump and tubing

hydrometer

b. Hatch and study brine shrimp or put other sea animals into the aquarium, such as sea horses or salt water fish.

c. Observe and record what sea animals eat.

d. Help students determine any patterns of behavior in the sea animals' lives. If yes, what are they?

8. Coral — Fragile Beauty

a. Point out to students that coral reefs look like plants, but they are actually animals. Explain that coral provides the ocean with lots of oxygen. In fact, one-half of the ocean's oxygen comes from coral. Coral is very fragile. A diver swimming past coral can kill it by brushing it with his or her fins. Coral grows extremely slowly—a small piece can take as long as a hundred years to grow. Encourage the students to find out the number of different varieties of coral and where the majority of coral can be found.

b. Explain to students that the ocean's coral is being destroyed at an alarming rate. Pollution is one cause and harvesting coral for jewelry is another. Invite students to find out exactly how pollution and other activities are destroying the ocean's coral. Challenge the students to think about what can be done to stop coral destruction. Encourage students to find out where the coral population is in the most danger of extinction. Ask students to present their findings to the class.

9. Murals of Ecosystems

a. Give students large sheets of white butcher paper, approximately 4 ft. x 5 ft. Invite students to create a display of an ocean or wetlands ecosystem they have been researching.

b. Encourage students to show the interdependence of the plants and animals in their ecosystem murals. Pictures of plants and animals can be found in wildlife magazines or bird, plant, and fish reference books. Encourage the students to carefully plan out their murals to accurately depict their ocean or wetlands ecosystems. Display the murals in the hallway outside the classroom.

10. Writing Letters

Encourage students to write for information about an ecosystem they are researching. For information about the oceans and other wetlands, the problems they face, and what can be done to protect them, students can write to:

American Shore and Beach Preservation
Association
P. O. Box 279
Middletown, CA 95461

Barrier Island Coalition
122 East 42nd Street, Suite 4500
New York, NY 10168

Center for Marine Conservation
1725 De Sales NW, Suite 500
Washington, DC 20036
202-429-5609

Adopt-a-Beach Program
The Seattle Aquarium
Pier 59
Waterfront Park
Seattle, WA 98101

Clean Water Action
1320 18th St. NW, 3rd Floor
Washington, DC 20036
202-457-1286

America's Clean Water Foundation
750 First St. NE, Suite 911
Washington, DC 20002
202-898-0902

11. Debates on Using Our Oceans

a. Invite students to participate in a debate on how the Earth's oceans should be used. Two or three students should take the "pro" position and two or three should take the "con."

b. Hold a class meeting to discuss how to prepare for a debate. Students should locate information on the topic using books and magazines listed in the suggested reading section. Encourage students to decide on the points they want to make and organize the arguments supporting their point of view. Encourage students to make notes for their arguments on 3" x 5" index cards.

c. Assist students as needed to help locate information and organize the points they want to make.

d. Hold the debates for the entire class. You may want to invite other classes to the debates as well. Encourage the audience to ask questions of the debaters. Ask the students in the audience if the points that were made by the debaters helped them to form or change their opinions.

e. Begin the debate by presenting the following information to the audience:

> Many countries have set up a 200-mile exclusive economic zone around their coastlines. Within this zone, the countries can control fishing. Agreements can be made with other countries to prevent overfishing of the waters and depleting the number of fish. However, fish, whales, and dolphins do not stay in one place. They move from one country's area to another. In the oceans, there are no agreements and countries have different opinions on who owns the fish in these areas.

f. Choose one of these two opinions to present in the debate:

> In the open ocean, the fish, whales, and dolphins do not belong to anyone. Therefore, anyone may catch as many fish as they want.
>
> or
>
> In the open ocean, the fish, whales, and dolphins belong to everyone. Therefore, everyone should have a share of any profit that comes from selling them.

Forest Ecosystems

𝒯he activities in this section will help students become more aware of forests as an important ecosystem. Select one or two books or articles on forests to share with the class before students begin an activity.

1. Important and Interesting Information to Know

Write the following facts on cards and then post the cards around the classroom. Encourage discussion or debate on any or all of the statements.

- About 30% of the Earth's land is covered with natural forests.

- Forests are natural resources and are vital to all living things.

- Trees absorb carbon dioxide, produce oxygen, prevent erosion, and help build the soil.

- Trees provide homes and food for birds, insects, and animals and are sources of ingredients for medicines.

- There are four major types of forests—tropical rainforests, temperate rainforests, coniferous forests, and deciduous forests.

- It takes hundreds of years for the trees in a forest to become old growth.

- Tropical rainforests are self-sustaining systems producing their own nutrients and their own climate.

- About one-quarter of all prescription drugs come from rainforest plants. Many popular fruits also originate from tropical rainforests.

- Forests are being threatened by the activities of people. When forests are lost, all living things are affected.

- Most of the deforestation has taken place during the 20th century.

2. Studying a Wooded Area Ecosystem

To study a forest ecosystem, sponsor a field trip to a wooded area. You will need the following materials:

4 stakes

enough rope to mark an area 9 ft. x 9 ft.

brightly colored flags or pieces of cloth to mark the stakes

a 10-foot tape measure

wildflower, plant, and tree identification books

journals and pencils for recording information

graph paper and clipboard

camera (optional)

a. Before starting this activity, it is important to remind students to wear long pants, long-sleeved shirts, shoes, socks, and gloves. Explain to the students the importance of not damaging the wooded area you will be working in. Have students mark off a section of woods 9 ft. x 9 ft. Drive the stakes into the corners of the area and mark the perimeter with rope or twine. Tie flags or pieces of cloth around each stake to clearly mark the area.

b. Have students find the center of the marked area. Place the graph paper on the ground at this point. Students will draft the plant life of the area using the graph paper.

c. As a group, select a tree within the roped-off area. Ask several students to measure the tree's circumference. Then measure the distance from the center of the roped-off area to the tree. Draw a circle on the graph paper to show the placement of the tree. Write the name of the tree and its circumference in the circle. Draw a line from the center of the map to the tree and record the distance.

d. Repeat this process for every tree in the roped-off area.

e. Ask students to locate and count the shrubs and wildflowers and measure their distances from the center of the map as well. Students should decide on symbols for recording the shrubs, wildflowers, and other small plants. Encourage students to get an accurate count of all the different plant species.

f. Encourage students to carefully look for insects and other small animals in the grass, under rocks, stones, twigs, leaves, and other debris. Record animal life on the graph paper, too.

g. Gather some of the decomposing leaves. Very carefully pick up a few millipedes, spiders, centipedes, salamanders, and sow bugs. Be sure students wear gloves when collecting specimens. When the students have finished recording the locations of the plants, animals, and insects on their graph paper, carefully remove the stakes from the marked area.

h. When the students get back to the classroom, have them transfer the information they collected on their graph paper to a scaled map of the area.

i. Hold a class meeting so students can discuss what they learned from this exercise. Encourage students to consider the following questions:

What did they smell in the woods?

What sounds did they hear?

What textures did they feel?

What were some of the most interesting things they saw on the field trip to the woods?

3. The Rainforests

a. Divide the class into cooperative-working groups of four or five students. Each group will draw a large tree, such as a kapok tree, in the middle of a large piece of paper. Divide the paper into three sections—the canopy or upper section, the understory or middle section, and the forest floor. Encourage students to research the types of rainforest vegetation using nonfiction sources available in the classroom. Have the students draw the vegetation they might actually find in a rainforest around the tree on their papers.

b. Write the following list of rainforest plants and animals on the chalkboard. Ask each group to choose three or four topics from the list to research. Encourage the students to ask questions, such as where do ocelots live and what do they eat, and so on. When the research has been completed, have students place a drawing of their plants or animals on the rainforest tree where they would actually be found—canopy, understory, or forest floor. Ask the groups to write short reports on their plants and animals and share their reports with the class. If possible, hang the groups' pictures side by side, creating a long mural of a rainforest ecosystem.

toucan	jaguar	anteater
orchid	sloth	tapir
macaw	iguana	wild pig
butterfly	ocelot	bromeliad

4. The Children's Rainforest

Share the following true story with your class. Then encourage students to find out all they can about The Children's Rainforest from their local librarian, or contact the Rainforest Action Network. Describe how big the rainforest is, what types of plants and animals live there, and who takes care of it. Encourage students to think about what projects the class might do to contribute to the rainforest's preservation.

Several years ago, a small boy decided he'd like to do something on his own to help save the rainforests. He began baking cookies and doing other small projects to make money. His idea was to save enough money to buy a rainforest and preserve it from destruction. Soon other children in his school began to help him. They raised lots of money. Eventually, children all over the world contributed to the rainforest fund. And they really did buy a portion of the rainforest! It's called "The Children's Rainforest" and it's located in Costa Rica in Central America. Today, children and adults continue to contribute money to buy more and more acres to preserve a larger portion of rainforest each year.

For information on saving the rainforests, write to:

Rainforest Action Network
300 Broadway, Suite 28
San Francisco, CA 94133

---

5. Exploring the Ecosystem in a Rotting Log

As a class, search for a rotting log on the school grounds or near the school. Take along the following materials:

- magnifying glasses
- field guides
- a paring knife
- spoon or trowel
- container for soil
- white plastic tray
- students' journals and pencils
- camera (optional)

a. Divide the class into three groups. Explain to students the importance of causing the least amount of disruption to the log ecosystem as possible. This means gently handling the log, bark, insects, and so on. In this activity, each group will look at one part of the log. Group one will look at the bark, group two at the wood under the bark, and group three at the soil under the log. Remind students to make sketches and to write careful notes about their observations in their journals. Remind the students to wear gloves to participate in this activity.

b. Group One: Look for holes in the bark. Holes show that birds have been drilling in the bark for insects. Look for long tunnels in the bark. These are signs of insects and bark beetles. Look for examples of mold, mildew, moss, and lichens. With a strong magnifying glass, students may be able to see bacteria growing on the log as well.

c. Group Two: Carefully lift off a section of the bark. Students should see the wood alive with creatures, such as ants, termites, wood lice, and insect larvae.

d. Group Three: Gently roll the log over to see the life under the log. Look for sow bugs, spiders, mites, scorpions, beetles, and other insects. Watch the activities of these animals. Carefully return the log to its original position.

6. Making a Terrarium to Show the Ecosystem of a Woodland Floor

To make a terrarium to show the ecosystem of a woodland floor, you will need the following materials:

> large glass container with lid
>
> small amount of sand, gravel, bits of charcoal
>
> rich soil, enough to cover the bottom of the container with 4 inches
>
> common plants found in woods—mosses, ferns, lichens
>
> small piece of rotting wood for bacteria, molds, and other decomposing organisms
>
> earthworms, sow bugs, salamander, or frog

Procedure:

a. Layer sand and gravel on the floor of the container. Scatters bits of charcoal over the sand and gravel. Charcoal is porous and will absorb some of the gases that will naturally be produced inside the ecosystem.

b. Spread 4 inches of rich soil over the charcoal. This should support the roots of the plants.

c. Transplant the plants from a wooded area.

d. Add mosses, ferns, fungi, lichens, and a piece of rotting log.

e. Add worms, sow bugs, salamander, frog, and meal worms.

f. Water the terrarium just enough to keep the soil damp. Place the lid on the terrarium to keep the animals in and to sustain the water cycle.

g. Add water only when the top of the soil is completely dry.

7. Growing a Rainforest

To make a rainforest in the classroom, you will need the following materials:

aquarium to use as a terrarium

gravel, small charcoal pieces, and small stones

rich compost or soil

small tropical plants from a florist or a greenhouse, such as a coffee plant, orchid, fern, palm, and philodendron

Procedure:

a. Put a layer of charcoal and gravel on the bottom of the terrarium. Put a few stones in several locations around the terrarium to make the landscape more interesting.

b. Cover the bottom of the terrarium with several inches of compost or soil.

c. Water the soil and plant the plants.

d. Cover the terrarium with plastic wrap. Keep in a warm place out of direct sunlight.

e. Water the plants every few days. Watch the rainforest terrarium to see what happens. Encourage students to record their observations in their journals.

8. Writing Letters for Information

Encourage students to write for information about forest ecosystems.

American Forestry Association
1516 P. Street, NW
Washington, DC 20036
202-667-3300

Correspondence Division
National Wildlife Federation
1400 16th Street, NW
Washington, DC 20003

Rainforest Action Network
300 Broadway, Suite #28
San Francisco, CA 94133

9. Debates on Using Our Forests

a. Invite students to participate in a debate on how the Earth's forests should be used. Two or three students should take the "pro" position and two or three should take the "con."

b. Hold a class meeting to discuss how to prepare for a debate. Students should locate information on the topic using books and magazines listed in the suggested reading section. Encourage students to decide on the points they want to make and organize the arguments supporting their point of view. Encourage students to make notes for their arguments on 3" x 5" index cards.

c. Assist students as needed to help locate information and organize the points they want to make.

d. Hold the debates for the entire class. You may want to invite other classes to the debates as well. Encourage the audience to ask questions of the debaters.

e. Begin the debate by presenting the following information:

> Settlers in America cut down many forests to clear the land for agricultural crops. Now, developed countries, such as the United States and other European countries, are criticizing the underdeveloped countries for allowing their people to cut down the forests for the same purpose.

f. Choose one of these two opinions to present in the debate:

> All countries should have the right without objections from other countries to do what they want with their forests.
>
> or
>
> Developed nations must cooperate with developing countries to regulate the development of forests without destroying them.

Desert Ecosystems

The activities in this section will help students become aware of deserts as an important ecosystem. Select one or two books or articles on deserts to share with the class before students begin an activity.

1. Important and Interesting Information to Know

Write each of the following facts on cards and then post the cards around the classroom. Encourage discussion about one or more of the statements.

- About one-seventh of the Earth's land surface is desert. Due to environmental changes, the world's deserts are expanding.

- Many deserts receive less than 10 inches of moisture a year.

- Deserts can be located in very cold or very warm climates.

- Even though the desert is a harsh environment, many plants and animals adapt and even thrive in the hostile climate.

2. Visiting a Desert

a. If you live in a desert area, plan a field trip with the class to observe the plant and animal life that lives there. Take pictures of the interesting specimens you find and of the general landscape.

b. Ask students to sketch any flowers they see as well. Have students look closely to see if some plants grow near rocks or in rock crevices. Encourage students to draw pictures of the desert plants in their journals.

c. Have students feel the soil and notice the earth's color. The soil in the shade of a rock will be cooler than the soil in sunlight.

d. Watch and listen for animals and look for animal tracks. Many animals sleep during the day and hunt at night when it is cooler.

e. Make a scrapbook of the desert, using the photographs you take and the pictures the students draw. Have students write captions for the pictures and short informational articles.

3. Creating a Desert Terrarium

To make a desert terrarium, you will need the following materials:

     large glass container

     very sandy soil

     small rocks and gravel

     a few small cacti

     beetles, grasshoppers

     window screen to cover terrarium

     thorn-proof gloves

Procedure:

a. Place a layer of rocks and gravel in the bottom of the container. Then cover with sandy soil. Plant a few small cacti and water lightly. Be sure students wear thorn-proof gloves for this activity.

b. Add beetles and grasshoppers. Cover the terrarium with window screen. Observe the terrarium at different times of the day. Turn off the lights and see if the insects are more active. Many inhabitants of the desert sleep during the hot daytime hours and are active at night when the temperature drops. Release the insects after several days in the terrarium.

4. What's in a Hump?

Explain to students that camels have lived in the Arabian and Sahara deserts for thousands of years. Ask students to find out what makes camels so well-suited to the hot, dry environment. Help students find pictures and information about camels in the library or media center. Encourage students to find out how each of the following characteristics of camels make them perfect for life in the desert. Answers are provided for your convenience.

a. eyes (Because their eyes are positioned high on their heads, camels can see long distances. Their heavy eyelids and long eyelashes help keep blowing sand out of their eyes.)

b. feet (Their well-cushioned feet help keep these big animals from sinking into the sand. The padding on their feet helps protect their feet from the hot sand.)

c. hump (The hump is filled with fat and connective tissue to use for energy when food and water are scarce.)

d. diet (Camels aren't picky—they'll eat anything—and the two-humped camel can even drink salt water! The tough skin surrounding the camel's teeth allows it to eat spiny, prickly plants.)

e. water (Camels can drink up to 30 gallons of water at a time, but they won't drink at all if they aren't thirsty.)

f. long neck (This is another characteristic that helps camels see long distances.)

g. nose (Here's a good trick—their nostrils can close to keep out blowing sand.)

h. size and strength (Camels are real pack animals, with the ability to carry up to 1000 pounds and travel as far as 100 miles in one day.)

5. Desert Plant Survival Characteristics

Divide the class into small cooperative-working groups. Ask each group to choose one desert plant and find out the characteristics that help the plant survive in the desert. When students have finished their research, have them design a poster. Each poster should have a picture of the plant and explain one or two interesting survival characteristics.

Prairies and Grasslands Ecosystems

$\mathcal{T}$he activities in this section are designed to raise the students' awareness of prairies and grassland ecosystems. Select one or two books or articles on grasslands to share with the class before students begin an activity.

1. Important and Interesting Information to Know

Write the following facts on cards and then post the cards around the classroom. Encourage discussion or debate among the students.

- Grasslands, also known as prairies and savannas, are located throughout North America, South America, Asia, Africa, and Australia.

- Almost all of the native grasslands in the United States have been plowed under and changed into agricultural land.

- Grasslands and prairies are often viewed as large expanses of land covered with tall grasses.

- Prairies and grasslands do not receive enough precipitation to support large trees and too much precipitation for desert vegetation.

- Once herds of 200,000 bison roamed the prairies.

2. Visiting a Prairie or Grassland Preserve

a. If you live on the prairie, plan a field trip to visit a nature preserve near the school. Call the county or State Department of Natural Resources for more information. Many of the natural grasslands of North America have been plowed under for farming or for ranching. Encourage students to find out what is being done to protect natural grasslands. While visiting the preserve, encourage students to:

- Sit quietly in a grassland area and look and listen for different varieties of birds. Encourage students to identify the different bird species. Have students record their guesses in their journals. Ask a naturalist at the preserve to name the species of birds that make this grassland preserve their home. Invite the students to check their guesses.

- Identify the different plants and animals. Invite students to draw pictures of the animals and plants in their journals.

b. Give students time to jot down their observations, questions, and reflections in their journals. After returning to the classroom, discuss the students' observations and impressions of the grassland field trip.

3. Where Are the Grasslands?

a. Ask students to use the reference materials in the suggested reading section to help locate the following grasslands:

    California grasslands
    intermountain grasslands
    shortgrass prairie
    mixed prairie
    tallgrass prairie

b. After students have completed their research, ask them to write a short summary of the main characteristics of each type of grassland identified.

c. Invite students to research the types of problems threatening the different grassland regions. Identify which problems are related to environmental changes or human intervention. Discuss with the students why it is important to protect our nation's grasslands.

4. Writing Books

Encourage students to write and illustrate collections of poems and stories about the prairies or grasslands. Prior to writing, discuss the characteristics of the different grasslands, the varieties of wildlife, and the diverse climates. Invite the students to look back in their journals for observations and illustrations about the grasslands. If students are interested, they can write their own collections of stories or poems or combine their writing into a class book. Display the books in either the classroom library or in the media center.

Tundra Ecosystem

*T*he activities in this section will heighten the students' awareness of the tundra ecosystem. Select one or two books or articles on the tundra to share with the class before students begin an activity.

1. Important and Interesting Information to Know

Write the following facts on cards and then post the cards around the classroom. Encourage discussion about each statement.

- The plains of the Arctic Circle are called *the tundra*.

- The temperature range is less than 0° C most of the year and never rises above 10° C.

- A thin layer of soil covers the permafrost—below the surface the ground stays frozen all year long.

- Plants that thrive on the tundra in spring and summer must have shallow, but large, root systems in order to take advantage of the nutrients and water within the soil.

2. Roots Take Hold

a. Explain to students that plants in the tundra have large, shallow root systems because the ground is frozen under a thin layer of soil. To see how shallow roots grow, you'll need the following materials:

seeds	soil
small paper cups	paper towels

b. Soak the seeds in water until they begin to sprout. Fill paper cups about half full of soil and then transplant the sprouted seeds. Plant the seeds just below the surface of the soil. Leave the small growth above the soil. Place the cups in a sunny location and keep the soil moist. Watch the plants grow for a few weeks. Then gently remove one plant from the cup and brush off the soil from the roots. Point out the intricate pattern of roots that have grown in such a short time. Discuss how plant roots in the tundra might look, since the soil they grow in is not very deep.

3. The Arctic Tundra Animals

Invite students to find out which of the following animals migrate to the Arctic tundra and which ones live there all year long. Encourage students to select one animal or bird to research. Give each student a 5" x 7" index card for writing a description of his or her animal or bird. Have students draw pictures of their animals on another 5" x 7" index card. Display the cards in random order around the classroom. Encourage students to match the descriptions with the illustrations.

Arctic hare	caribou
ptarmigan	red fox
stoat	snowy owl
lynx	snow goose
musk ox	sandbill crane

4. Hibernating Hideaways

a. Explain to students that the temperature below the snow is three degrees centigrade or about seven degrees centigrade warmer than above the snow surface. While squirrels hibernate, weasels hunt lemmings in their burrows. Other animals survive on insects that live below the ground. Point out that hollow tunnels beneath the surface are sheltered from the wind and filled with trapped warm air that functions as insulation.

b. Invite students to research one or two of the following tundra animals: shrews, mice, stoats, voles, squirrels, and weasels. Ask students to find out how these animals spend the winter—in hibernation or scurrying through tunnels below the surface in search of food. Have students create a cut-away drawing of their findings. Show the frozen tundra above ground and the animals' life underground.

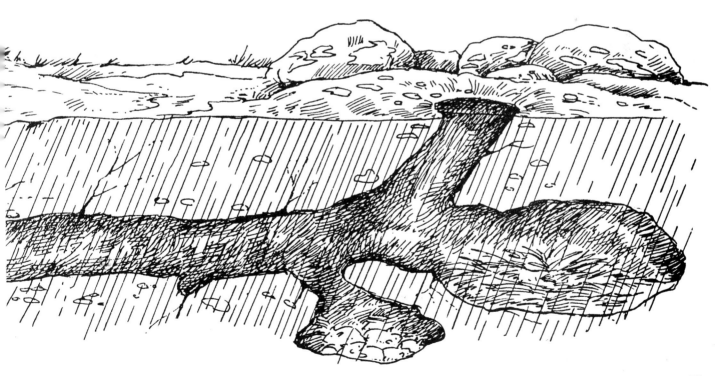

Food Chains and Food Webs—Who Eats What?

$\mathcal{T}$he activities in this section are designed to help increase students' **awareness** of food chains and food webs and the role they play in the **survival** of an ecosystem. Share information with the students about food **chains** and food webs from a variety of sources prior to beginning the activities.

1. Determining Prior Knowledge

a. Hold a class meeting to talk about students' favorite foods. After students have named the foods they like to eat, ask why eating is important. What would happen if students didn't eat? Be sure students understand they get essential energy from food. Ask students where they think their food comes from. For example, if students say their favorite food is a hamburger, where does the hamburger come from?

b. Put a small insect, such as a grasshopper, in a glass jar with air holes, but no food. Place the jar in a location where students can see it. Observe the insect specimen for a short period of time and then release it back into the environment. Hold a class discussion to talk about what the grasshopper needs to survive. Where does the grasshopper live? If the insect were in its natural habitat, what would it eat? If students do not know, help them find the answers in several reference books.

2. Constructing Food Chains and Webs

a. All animals can be divided into groups depending on what they eat. Those that eat plants only are called *herbivores*. Creatures that eat meat only are called *carnivores*. Animals or human beings that eat both plants and animals are called *omnivores*. Worms and cockroaches are called *decomposers* because they eat animal and plant materials that are normally discarded. Because of the decomposers, nothing is ever wasted.

b. Food webs, which are food chains that overlap, can be difficult to construct. Ask groups of students to construct a food web for the plants and animals in the ecosystems they have been studying.

c. Provide large sheets of butcher paper so students can show food relationships among the animals in their ecosystems. Have students draw the plants and animals, or use small pictures whenever possible, as a visual image of the ecosystem food web. Students should determine which animals are the producers, the herbivores, the carnivores, and the omnivores. Remind students to include human beings in their food webs, if appropriate.

wolf

coyote

deer

rabbit

green plants

3. Reinacting a Food Web

Explain to the students that they are going to create a food web using a yarn ball. Encourage students to name an organism from a food web that you have previously discussed, such as phytoplankton or grass. Begin the activity by throwing a ball of yarn to the student who is one of the first organisms in the food web. Have the student tell what he or she is, such as phytoplankton. This person then throws the yarn ball to the next person in the web, zooplankton or a salmon, for example. Continue up the food chain to the end. What's important is not getting all the organisms in the food web exactly in order, but understanding that all organisms are somehow connected. While the students are still holding onto the yarn, explain how a change that affects one part of the food web can change an entire ecosystem. For example, if a pollutant poisons most of the fish in an area, all the creatures that depend on fish for food are affected. To demonstrate this, have all the students who represent animals that eat fish drop their pieces of yarn. Point out the disruption to the food web. Challenge students to think of other examples of food webs that have been altered due to human changes to the environment as well.

4. Newsletters to Parents and Other Classes

a. As a group, have students decide what information they would like to tell their parents and students in other classes about the ecosystems they have been studying. List the ideas on a sheet of paper.

b. Have students list ways to communicate their ideas—news articles, cartoons, poems, stories, essays, and puzzles. Encourage students to volunteer for at least one of the projects listed.

c. Several students can serve as newsletter editors to help students with clarity, punctuation, capitalization, and spelling as they complete their newsletter projects.

Important Words to Know

canopy – treetops, the upper layer of a forest

carnivore – an animal whose main source of food is meat

conifer – an evergreen tree or shrub that has needles instead of broad leaves and cones instead of flowers

consumer – organisms that eat green plants or other organisms

continental shelf – underwater ledge that runs along many coastlines

deciduous trees – trees that lose their leaves and fruit at the end of the growing season

ephemeral – plants and flowers that grow for a very short period of time after it has rained

epiphytes – are air plants; their roots dangle in the air and grow in the cracks of tree branches

estuaries – places where freshwater rivers flow from inland areas into the salty waters of the ocean

food chain – describes how living things depend on each other for food; a food chain usually includes a plant, a plant eater or herbivore, and one or more meat eaters or carnivores

food web – food chains that overlap

herbivores – animals that only eat plants

interdependence – the way plants and animals depend on each other for food, habitat, or reproduction

omnivores – animals that eat both plants and animals

pond – small area of still water

species – a group of plants or animals that look alike and behave in similar ways

temperate forests – found between the very cold polar areas and the very hot tropical areas; temperate forests contain mostly deciduous trees

understory – the second level of trees in a forest; smaller trees that live in the shade of the larger trees of the canopy

Our Ecosystems © 1993 Fearon Teacher Aids